Disney
Winnie the Pooh

How Did You Make
That Web?

Pooh was searching for his favorite honeypot, turning his house all topsy-turvy, when he first saw the spider web.

He sat down on the floor beside the web and looked at it for a long time. A small spider was walking back and forth across some sticky threads. Pooh watched and wondered with great delight. Then he asked the question that he had been wondering about. "How did you make that web?"

Suddenly, Pooh heard someone knocking at his door. When he opened it, Piglet was standing there.

"Hello, Piglet," said Pooh, inviting his friend inside. "Please come in. I want to show you something."

"What is it, Pooh?" asked Piglet.

Pooh pointed to the web on his wall.

"Look at this spider web," he said. "It has been taking the spider a long time to weave it, because he is a very careful builder."

"Let's watch and see," said Piglet.

Pooh and Piglet studied the spider. It was using silky threads from its own body to make the web.

"Oh, isn't that clever, Piglet!" Pooh said with a laugh. "I guess animals build with parts of their body."

"Yes, that *must* be how animals build," agreed Piglet.

Just then, a small mouse ran past them and scurried into a hole in the wall. The mouse was carrying a tiny piece of paper in its mouth.

Pooh and Piglet peeked inside the hole, but it was too dark in there to see anything.

"Oh, dear!" said Piglet, looking at the mess on Pooh's floor.
Pooh saw that there were tiny pieces of paper everywhere. "Why do you suppose he did that?"

The little mouse peeked out, raced across the floor, picked up a piece of cotton, and carried it back inside.

"Oh, look, Pooh!" Piglet cried. "I think that mouse is using the paper and cotton to build a nest in the hole!"

Pooh nodded and smiled.

"I suppose animals build by using parts of their bodies *and* things they find lying around," he said.

"Yes, you must be right," Piglet agreed. "They use any old thing they can stuff into a nest and pile up any old way."

Suddenly, Piglet heard a fluttering sound outside Pooh's window. He pointed to a bird flying by.

"That bird is carrying twigs and leaves up into the tree," he said.

Pooh saw Owl coming in for a landing.

"Here comes Owl," he called. "Perhaps he can tell us what the bird is building."

"I'd be happy to," replied Owl. "The bird is building a nest for her babies."

"Hmmm," said Pooh. "It seems to me that some animals use something from their bodies to build with, or they use whatever they can find to make into a messy nest...."

"Or," added Owl, "they use things in nature that they can carefully weave into a proper sort of nest."

"Either way," said Piglet, "there is certainly a lot of building going on."

"Let's see who else is building something in the Wood," said Pooh. So the three friends went for a walk. When they reached the Sandy Pit, Piglet saw a colony of ants building a cone-shaped anthill.

Pooh watched the busy ants going in and out of the anthill. "Hmmm," he said thoughtfully. "There's something else that animals build with—sand."

"Some animals are busy builders," said Piglet. "They build with things their bodies make, or things they find lying about that they can pile up any old way...."

"Or things in nature that they carefully weave together," said Owl.
"Or with sand," Piglet added proudly.

Pooh looked down and patted his stomach.

"All this thinking, watching, and building is giving me a rumbly tummy," he said. "I could do with a smackerel of honey."

"And I know just where we'll find some," said Owl. "Let's go see the very thing that bees know how to build. Follow me."

So the three friends went off to find a beehive.

Pooh, Piglet, and Owl soon found some busy bees inside a tree hollow. It was full of honeycomb that the bees had built using wax from their own bodies.

"Sort of like the spider's silky threads," said Piglet.

"Exactly," replied Owl. "Except the bees use honeycomb to hold their honey."

"Perhaps I can build something useful, too," Pooh said.

And with that, Pooh looked down at the ground. He scooped up some mud and shaped it into a bowl. Then he covered the inside and outside with leaves and twigs until he made a sort of basket. *Drip, drip, drip!* The golden honey from a beehive dripped down, filling up Pooh's basket.

"I may not be able to spin a web or build a nest or a sandy hill or make honey," said Pooh happily. "But I can build something useful, too. I can build a basket to hold my honey whenever I'm away from home without a honeypot."

At last, Pooh dipped his paw into his honey basket.

"Ahhh," he sighed and smacked his lips. "For me, home is where the honey is!"

Build a Web

Most animals build what they need to survive. Some create elaborate homes for their young, while others devise ways to trap food or store their food—such as honeycomb.

A spider builds a web in order to trap the food it needs to survive. Spiders produce sticky threads in their bodies and use them to weave webs. Spiders within the same species weave webs that are similar, but different kinds of spiders weave different kinds of webs.

Look closely at a spider web. The design and pattern is pretty amazing, isn't it?

This hands-on spider web activity utilizes discovery, observation, comparing and contrasting—skills that help young children learn.

Here's how to make your own spider web:

Step 1: Search for spider webs and compare them. Don't get too close or touch the spider.

Step 2: Use yarn, heavy string, or sticky masking tape to build your spider web. Criss-cross the materials along chair legs or other frame.

Step 3: To show how spiders trap their prey, cut masking tape into strips and roll them up. Make sure that the sticky side of the tape is on the outside.

Step 4: Attach cut-out pictures or toy models of insects onto the masking-tape ball and let it "land" on the sticky web.